PLASTIC POLLUTION

Reduce it in 8 Simple Ways

ROWENA CARO-BENAVIDES

Plastic Pollution: Reduce it in 8 Simple Ways
Philippine Copyright © 2019 by Rowena C. Benavides

ISBN: 9781702204873

October 2019

Request for information should be addressed to:
Rowena C. Benavides
College of Forestry and Environmental Studies
MSU-Maguindanao
Dalican, Datu Odin Sinsuat, Maguindanao
Email: weng.caro@gmail.com

CONTENTS

Acknowledgement

This work is not possible without our Almighty God who provides all wisdom for me to pursue and consistently write to bring this message and enhance the understanding of the people.

To my mentor Ms. Sha Nacino, who shares valuable and detailed guide to write this book.

To Mindanao State University – Maguindanao for allowing me to have a valuable time to write and finish this book

To my ever supportive editors Dr. Virgencita B. Caro and Ms.Krystel Shane Balondo-Caro.

To my siblings: Gabriel, Raquel, Rafael and Vincent; nieces and nephews: Alfeah, AJ and MG who support and offer prayers to persistently write in times when

I don't feel like writing.

To my husband: Jerwin and two lovely children Alexander and Nicole who is so patient and understanding.

To them I awe my gratitude

INTRODUCTION

As I was drafting our research paper about the alternatives to single use plastics, I read a lot about the dangerous effects of single use plastics in the environment and in our health.

I felt this heaviness in my heart. I wanted to spread the message using simple terms and not in the scientific jargons.

A small voice was telling me to write a book. A book about the dangers of single use plastics and how we can contribute to the solution using simple and understandable terms.

This is my way to inspire the youth that even at their very young age they can do something for the environment.

I want to touch many hearts to make them feel the urgency of an environmental problem. As individuals, we can stop or minimize our consumption of single use plastics.

Hopefully, this will prompt the youth to move in their own ways to cut single-use plastic consumption.

I am writing this book because I want that we will live in a better and healthier environment.
This is my way of serving mother-nature: spread my knowledge about the dangers of single use plastics, and show the world how we can contribute to the solution.

WHAT ARE PLASTICS?

Plastics are defined by the United Nations Environment Programme (2018) as lightweight, hygienic and resistant material which can be moulded in a variety of ways and utilized in a wide range of applications.
In today's lifestyle, plastics play a major role in everyday life.

Most of these plastics are designed to be used only once and then thrown away.

We use it every moment in almost all our lives. We reach the point where we cannot live without it.

They are only used in minutes, like plastic straws and unnecessary plastic packaging.

On the average, plastic straws are only used for 12 minutes.

These plastic packaging materials comprise almost half of all the plastics produced in the entire world. These packaging materials are usually unnecessary and are only used to make the product appealing to the consumers.

Huge packaging of coffee brands is an alarming example to check. These coffee products can be contained in smaller packs.
These sachet packages are made of a thin film of plastic with aluminium in a sandwich laminate form.

A research conducted by GAIA 2019 says that 55 % of single use plastic wastes are branded sachets. This shows how much multinational corporations have control over us. This trend of plastic use like packaging and other short-lived applications is unsustainable.

Majority of plastics today came from fossil fuels. This serve as the primary source of plastic production due to its cheaper cost.

Plastics are formed by extracting crude and natural gas from the environment. These fossil fuels are then sent to refineries.

At the refineries, polymerization followed, where a catalyst is added to link the molecules together to make polymers called resins. These structures are responsible for the flexibility of plastics. It can then be moulded into different products. Most of these products are disposable.

These disposable plastics are called single-use plastics.

The moment we wake up in the morning, we are serving ourselves coffee in a sachet. We hit the shower and use shampoos in a sachet.
We cleanse our faces with facial foams with micro plastic beads in sachets. Sachets are thrown here and there.

During weekends, we wash our clothes using sachet powdered soaps. Rinse them with the sweet scent of sachet fabric conditioners.

Our consumption of these sachet items has become a way of life. This is because of their outright availability, and the convenience it offers for budgeted consumption of goods.

I cannot blame our patronage of using these products. It is perceived as an affordable solution to our financial budgets, as it is being portrayed.
Our way of using single use plastic has led us to a waste accumulation beyond what we can manage in our lifetime.
Plastic problem must be addressed at source. These corporations must be held accountable, to stop the enormous amount of waste.

In our search for solutions to plastic pollution, brought by plastic sachet items, individual consumer choice will make an impact.

SINGLE USE PLASTICS ARE HARMFUL TO THE ENVIRONMENT

I was watching the news about the devastating effects of typhoon Karding.
There was this huge volume of trash scattered all over the streets. The sudden rise of water level brought all kinds of plastic trash back

to the street causing heavy traffic. People were walking in the flooded street with floating plastic wastes. The said typhoon produced huge amount of water. This water came rushing towards the sea. But as it makes its way to the oceans, plastic wastes were clogging the drainage and the rivers.
Different forms of plastics are occupying our drainage and sewerage causing blockage. Due to the drainage congestion water could not go down.
Instead, it makes its way to other areas, making and intensifying the flood.

The flood destroys properties and hampers the activity of the community.

Aside from a flooded street, the stagnant water becomes a breeding ground for mosquitoes and other rodents.

It can lead to another threat of mosquito and rodent borne diseases such as dengue, malaria and leptospirosis.

Plastics can also destroy the aesthetic beauty of a place.
In South Africa, before they ban the use of single use plastic bags, there were so many plastic bags littering their environment. A joke circulates that the new national flower is the plastic bag.

This is how single use plastic has damaged our environment and intensified calamities.

Our indiscriminate and improper disposal of garbage is causing us all these troubles.

SINGLE USE PLASTICS ARE HARMFUL TO WILDLIFE

In MSU-Maguindanao, the university where I teach, we have these yearly field trips. One of our destinations is the D'Bone Collector Museum Inc in Davao City.

One of the highlights of the museum display is the huge bone of whale.

According to the museum facilitator, the whale was found dead in the shores of Compostela Valley, Davao del Sur.

The whale underwent an autopsy, led by Darrell Blatchley, director of D'Bone Collector Museum Inc.

It was found out that the stomach of the whale contains 40 kilograms of plastics.

Imagine being able to eat a whole plastic bag? The thought of it makes me vomit.

In Indonesia, a sperm whale died with 6 kilograms of plastic waste in its stomach.

Several recorded incidents from our neighbouring countries found dead whales, albatrosses, turtles, and other marine creatures with stomachs full of plastics.
In Thailand, a whale was found dead after swallowing more than 80 plastic bags. Green turtle died the same way in 2018.

Marine birds got entangled with these plastics.
These are some of the thousands of stories of marine deaths. These animals perceived plastic bags as real food.

The reported cases only portrayed a small percentage of marine creatures death.

Life forms died without us noticing them and wake up one day that we already lost these treasures we once have.

These are clear proofs of how grave plastic pollution is. It affects our wildlife, especially the aquatic organisms.

The worst thing, plastics are so durable that organisms cannot shake these off out of their bodies.
Plastic bags thrown in the oceans and eaten by sea

creatures cause death to wildlife.

There is nothing wrong with having small and short pleasures, like sipping drinks or licking lolly pops, but we must reconsider not to use plastic straws or plastic lollypop sticks.

There are products that offer the same pleasure but made of eco-friendly materials.

SINGLE USE PLASTICS ARE HARMFUL TO HUMAN HEALTH

Plastics contain harmful toxic chemicals that could affect the human health. Some of these toxic chemicals are styrene and benzene. These chemicals are known for their carcinogenic potential that could affect human organs.

One source of plastic that enters into our body is the microplastic from the table salts.

According to the World Health Organization (WHO), adults should consume less than 5 g of salts a day. This amount of salt consumption, approximately, we can eat 1,000 microplastic particles in a year from table salt.
Hence, microplastics becomes a threat to human health due to its capacity to absorb persistent organic pollutants.

Microplastics are also detected in both tap and bottled water a thing we can't live without.

Aside from the salt and bottled water, many studies have shown that toxins in Styrofoam can seep in to the food, especially when in contact with heat which is hazardous to human health.

A study published in Environmental Health Perspective conducted by the Tokyo Metropolitan Research Laboratory of Public Health (2001) shows that human breast tumour cells increase when exposed to styrene gas from food containers.

HOW CAN WE CONTRIBUTE TO THE SOLUTION?

HALF A BILLION
OF PLASTIC
STRAWS ARE USED
AND DISCARDED
EVERY DAY.

-latimes.com

STOP USING PLASTIC STRAWS

As I was scanning through youtube, I came across a video of a turtle with its nose pinned by a straw. The video hit me right on the spot. I saw the turtle's tears running down its checks and its blood rolling down from its nose.

The straw looks like it's been there for quite a while and is embedded in the turtles flesh.

The turtle was in dire pain that no animal should ever have to endure it.

The way I see it, the turtle is struggling in excruciating pain, suffering distress caused by irresponsible disposal of plastic waste.

I wonder if the turtle wishes to have hands to save itself and pull the straw out of its nose. I wonder how agonizing it is for this poor creature to breathe just to survive.

The straw that got into the turtle's nose is just one of the millions of straws we throw away after minutes of use.

Millions of plastic straws entered our environment every single day. These straws are used for around 15-20 minutes and then are thrown away.
To tackle this problem the "straw upon request" or ban plastic straws is advised. This is a way to solve this tremendous amount of waste, where most of the time is left for the future generations to deal with.

This is only one example of the consequences of our scrupulous use of plastic straws.

That is only one of the many marine organisms which become a victim of our short time convenience.

◆ ◆ ◆

Action steps

Though a lot of food establishments have vowed to "no to plastic straws", you can also buy your own reusable straw that you can carry with you anywhere.

17

Million barrels of oil are used in producing bottled water each year.

MSKL Watershed Installation (2009)

USE REUSABLE WATER BOTTLE

I have this green small water bottle that I carry to school every day.

One time when I was about to go home, I ordered dinner for take-out and place the drinks into my water bottle.

I took a bus, ate my dinner and I placed the water bottle on a small corner of my seat. When I arrived and step out of the bus, I wanted to sip a little water and remembered that I left my water bottle on my seat.

Water bottles are very important, not only when we travel but also in our everyday activities.

I always carry my reusable water bottle for several reasons.

First, I don't want to add more waste from single use plastic bottle. By refilling my reusable water bottle, I can help cut plastic waste dumped into the trash.

Second, it's better for my health. Studies show that disposable plastic bottles are made of PET (Polyterephthlate) plastics which leach toxic chemicals known as antimony into water. Antimony is hazardous to human health. It can cause headache and gastro intestinal disturbances upon exposure. Third, It will help me save money. Imagine, a refill for a glass of water will only cost me a peso while a bottled water will cost me for around 10 pesos. I am saving a hundred percent for every buy.

One reusable water bottle will last for years of usage. This is a huge lap in my goal to contribute for sustainability and zero-waste initiatives. Having only one bottle to maintain will remove clutter in my physical space. It also allows me to value the things that I do have.

Action Steps

Make sure you have your own water bottle. Buy yourself a handy and durable water bottles to keep

you hydrated all day long.
Bring along your bottle anywhere either in school or in the office.

"EVERY YEAR,120 BILLION PIECES OF DISPOSABLE PLASTIC CUTLERY ARE DISCARDED IN INDIA"

says the founder of Bakeys Food Pvt Ltd

treehugger.com

STOP USING DISPOSABLE SPOON AND FORK

I travel for 10-15 hours every week. Having an extra item in my bag like the reusable spoon and fork is often not a priority. So I ended up using these disposable spoon and fork.

Statistics says that if every Filipino will use one set of disposable spoon and fork once a week, will total to at least 104 spoons and forks in a year.

There are at least 105 million Filipinos. This makes it 920 million plastic utensils discarded into the environment.

If we cut this disposable spoon and fork in the mainstream, it will be a huge help to reduce plastic waste in the environment.

Aside from reducing plastics in the environment. There are other healthy reasons why bringing my own spoon and fork is worth the extra weight in my bag.

It helps me avoid certain diseases.

Having my own utensils, I don't have to worry if the utensil I am using is sanitized and of who used these utensils beforehand.

It helps me save valuable resources, like fossil fuels, the main raw material in the production of disposable utensils.
Finally, it helps me reduce the plastic waste in the environment.

Action steps

Buy yourself a set of reusable spoon and fork to carry with you wherever you go.

Eat with friend and tell them the benefits of bringing your own utensils. In this way, you can spread the message.

ONE MILLION PLASTIC BAGS ARE USED EVERY MINUTE

Matanglawin

USE REUSABLE ECO-BAGS

I was in the supermarket doing my usual weekly grocery.

That afternoon, there was a long queue of customers so it took me quite a while to reach the counter to pay for my items. When it was my turn to pay, I was surprised when the packer grabbed some brown paper bags to separate my grocery items. The cashier asked me if I am willing to pay for extra 45 pesos for that durable, reusable and biodegradable bag. It left me with no choice the brown paper bags support my canned goods. So I decided to pay and buy one.

Off course, I always thought of bringing with me my eco-bag.

I always thought of bringing an eco-bag every time I do such weekly task. Unfortunately, I often forget to bring one. I only remember it when I am lining up at the grocery counter.

Now, I always feel the strong urge to carry with me my eco-bag. Especially that I have to pay every time I failed to bring it with me, with or without doing my grocery stuff.

Action steps

Give a friend an eco-bag. This way, you can motivate them to use eco bags instead of utilizing plastic bags whenever they buy.

Most of the time, when going to the grocery store we always have our list of items to buy. To refrain from forgetting the eco-bag, add it on the list until it becomes a must have before going to buy anything.

After using it, fold it and store it in a clean container. It will be convenient to grab one when going to the store again.

164 MILLION PIECES OF PLASTIC SACHETS ARE USED IN THE PHILIPPINES DAILY.

Global Alliance for Incinerator Alternatives

REFRAIN FROM BUYING SACHET ITEMS

The time I started working and have my own money to spend, through better budgeting, I am learning to make both ends meet.

Whenever I am going to get my weekly supplies of groceries, I make sure to shop for my necessary needs that would last to the next payday.

To do this, I often ended up in picking sachet items, like shampoos, powdered soap, fabric conditioner, coffee, milk and soy sauce, even beauty products like moisturizers and facial cleansers.

But as I weigh the benefits versus the environmental cost, the environmental damage is way beyond the benefit of saving a little money.

The small penny that I have saved is nothing compared to the cost of restoration.

As my understanding deepened, I shifted to buying bulk items one at a time. It turns out to be a lot cheaper compared to buying them in sachets. Hence, I save more in buying in bulk compared to purchasing in sachets.

Almost all our necessities are items, packed in plastic sachets.

Single-use sachets that include shampoo, toothpaste, detergents, and coffee are means of the low income communities to enjoy quality products.
Yet, greater impact on the reduction of plastic sachets lies in the hands of the government. Creation of policies followed by strict implementation will help decrease plastic wastes.

Real solutions and significant reductions in single use plastic waste must start from where these plastic sachets come from.

Action Steps

When shopping or buying your needed items, choose products packed in natural materials.

Try to avoid products with too much packaging.

As much as possible, buy in bulk.

STYROFOAM
CONTAINERS
CAN TAKE UP
TO1,000 YEARS
TO DECOMPOSE

STOP USING FOAMED PLASTICS AS FOOD CONTAINERS

When I was younger, whenever there were celebrations or gatherings, food was served in a buffet.

Today, foods are packed inside the foamed plastic container.

After consuming the food, remains the huge waste of single use styrofoam container.

The mere sight of the huge volume of garbage is so disheartening.

Besides, fast food take outs are using Styrofoam as containers for food and drinks.

Every time I need to buy a take-out food, I make sure that the container is either paper or reusable container.

I also make sure to carry with me my reusable food container.

Studies show that toxic chemicals in Styrofoam containers can transfer to food and drinks.
These toxic chemicals are known to be cancer causing toxins.

Action steps

Choose establishments in your vicinity that do not use single use plastics. Tell your friends about these establishments. Shop and dine in these type of enterprise.

As a consumer you can demand from these food establishments to use reusable utensils, or provide customers with similar options.

Patronize caterers that use ceramic or glass wares.

Carry your own reusable food containers.

GLOBALLY, 560,000 TONS OF GUM EACH YEAR IS CHEWED.

Imfeld, T., 1999. Chewing gum—facts and fiction: a review of gum-chewing and oral health.

SKIP CHEWING GUMS

E arly this year, we went to Dumaguete City to attend my brother's graduation.

We flew from Cagayan de Oro airport to Dumaguete.

I sat with my little girl so I had to lift the arm of the chair to sit closer to her.

I leaned my back on the chair for quite a while to rest. When the plane landed. I stood up and noticed something sticky on my shirt's shoulder.

It was a chewing gum. Some negligent person had discarded a chewing gum on the plane's chair.
What makes it worst, it was the new t-shirt given to me by my mom from her trip in Thailand.

I was really pissed off.

That is why I hate gum, but what I hate the most are

those who chew gum and dispose it irresponsibly.

In exemption to some, most of the bubble gums are made of polyethylene and polyvinyl acetate.

These plastic chemicals have shown to cause tumors in lab rats.

◆ ◆ ◆

Action Step

If possible skip chewing gum.

When chewing a gum, make sure to dispose it properly so it would not cause harm to other people.

If possible use the biodegradable gums or simply stop buying gums.

150 ML OF
THE BEAUTY
PRODUCTS
COULD CONTAIN
BETWEEN 137,000
AND 2.8 MILLION
MICRO PARTICLES

Richard Thompson

AVOID PRODUCTS THAT USE MICROBEADS

Every day, I wash my face with soap. Once in a while, I use facial foam to cleanse my face deeply, especially when pimples start to pop up.

I choose facial foams with extra cleansing ability by having microbeads in it. These micro beads are added along with other ingredients in the cleanser.

Little did I know that these micro-beads are made of plastic materials. That are hazardous to the environment, wildlife, and human health.

These micro-beads are not only found in facial foams but also in other products like face soaps, body washes, toothpastes, lip glosses and nail polishes.

A single tube of facial cleanser contains at least 356,000 microbeads. This is one of the great innovation of beauty products for achieving an abrasive effect.

These micro-beads are so small with size less than millimetres. Approximately as small as pin head and often end up in our rivers and oceans.

Once they are washed out and reached bodies of water. These micro-beads absorb the cancer-causing persistent organic pollutants in the environment. The long-lasting toxic chemicals like pesticides, motor oil, etc.
These toxic coated beads move up to the food chain once they are eaten by fish and other marine organisms.

If ingested by animals, these microbeads deprive the creatures of needed nutrients. These lodge in their digestive tract causing pain, inability to eat and eventual death.

There is no clear evidence as to what harm these microbeads can cause in human health but surely they are making their way back to our plates.

As the saying goes, what comes around goes around.

Action Step

Avoid product that uses micro-beads.

Opt for beauty products that are made of natural and biodegradable ingredients like ground nut shells, salt or sugar crystals.
Read the label. Make sure the term "micro-beads" is not around.

CONCLUSION

P lastic is still an extremely valuable resource. An excellent material for almost anything. But it is used unscrupulously.

We exploited it thru our own "throw here and there" culture.

Responsible use of plastic material will take us miles in keeping the environment, animals and humans healthy.

If our current rate of plastic consumption will continue and without doing anything to regulate the single use plastics, a day will come that it will cover the entire earth surface. Many said that, in a few years, there will be more plastic than fish in our oceans.

Our individual choice of consumer goods can drive the market to have organic goods and packaging.

If there are enough number of consumers who will demand to different supermarkets and enterprises that they will collect back the plastic they issue, they might make the necessary actions and recycle it.

If we don't buy individually packed plastic goods, then business might not sell it as well.

In our hands, lies the answers to our current problems in plastic pollution.

500 billion disposable cups are consumed every year.

Development of chemicals for use should involve an interaction between biologist and chemist. If these had been in place 50 years ago it would have prevented the development of harmful chemicals.

Plastics will play a significant role as we move forward to the future. It is increasingly used in medical applications. It's light weight component for the new Beoing 787 will reduce fuel consumption.

But our current production strategies, use and disposals are unsustainable. It poses severe threat to environment, wildlife and human health.

Solutions are available through combined actions. For individuals through appropriate use and disposal. Industries should adopt green chemistry, material reduction and design products appropriate for reuse. The government and policy makers should set standards for appropriate product labelling. And incentivised those that reduce or cut their single-use plastics.

ABOUT THE AUTHOR

I am Rowena C. Benavides.

A mother, wife, teacher, writer and a traveller.

A teacher of Environmental Science at MSU-Maguindanao for more than a decade already.

A blogger for the environment.

My mission is to help raise awareness and motivate people to action for environmental appreciation, protection and conservation.

My website: https://angkalikasan.com/
My facebook fan page: fb.com/Ang-Kalikasan